FORERU[...]
FROM T[...]RESS

Origina[...]**ip**

FORERUN[...] T0154956 [...]cess series of break-
through [...] h ideas and finished
books, Forerunners draws on scholarly work initiated in notable
blogs, social media, conference plenaries, journal articles, and the
synergy of academic exchange. This is gray literature publishing:
where intense thinking, change, and speculation take place in
scholarship.

Ian Bogost
The Geek's Chihuahua: Living with Apple

Grant Farred
Martin Heidegger Saved My Life

John Hartigan Jr.
Aesop's Anthropology: A Multispecies Approach

Reinhold Martin
Mediators: Aesthetics, Politics, and the City

Shannon Mattern
Deep Mapping the Media City

Jussi Parikka
The Anthrobscene

Steven Shaviro
No Speed Limit: Three Essays on Accelerationism

Sharon Sliwinski
Mandela's Dark Years: A Political Theory of Dreaming

Mandela's Dark Years

Mandela's Dark Years
A Political Theory of Dreaming

Sharon Sliwinski

University of Minnesota Press

MINNEAPOLIS

Published by the University of Minnesota Press, 2015
111 Third Avenue South, Suite 290
Minneapolis, MN 55401-2520
http://www.upress.umn.edu

The University of Minnesota is an equal-opportunity educator and employer.

Excising the political from the life of the
mind is a sacrifice that has proven costly.

—TONI MORRISON, *Playing in the Dark*

Contents

The Prisoner's Nightmare

ONE GRAY DAY NOT SO LONG AGO, I found myself wandering around an airport bookstore. I suspect you are familiar with the kind of place; it was one of those brightly lit kiosks with tiered banks of magazines and pocket-sized paperbacks that are designed to capture the attention of the jet-lagged traveler. I browsed for a while and was about to leave empty-handed when Nelson Mandela's smiling face caught my eye. I had wanted to read his autobiography, *Long Walk to Freedom,* for some time, and when the venerable leader died at the end of 2013, the desire was revived. I purchased the hefty volume and headed off to my departure gate.

Mandela's autobiography begins, predictably enough, with the story of his childhood. Places and names are significant to his narrative. He was given the name Rolihlahla at his birth (which means "pulling the branches off the tree," read "troublemaker"). When he was sent away to school at age seven, he acquired a clan name, Madiba, and his first teacher, in accordance with colonial custom, gave him a Christian name, Nelson. After a rebellious youth, Mandela eventually made his way to the University of the Witwatersrand, where he slowly worked toward a degree (repeatedly failing his qualifying exams) as the only black law student.

You probably know the basic outline of what happened next: as a young lawyer practicing in Johannesburg in the 1940s, he joined the African National Congress (ANC) Party. In 1951, after the National Party took power, he helped organize the Defiance Campaign in response to the new apartheid laws. When the ANC's nonviolent tactics were met with violent reprisals from the Afrikaner government, Mandela began advocating for a different strategy. In 1961, he publicly stated, "If the government reaction is to crush by naked force our non-violent struggle, we will have to reconsider our tactics."[1] The young leader suffered a series of bans, served several jail sentences, and eventually cofounded the militant wing of the ANC, Umkhonto we Sizwe (or MK). He went underground and undertook guerrilla warfare training but was eventually captured and tried at the infamous Rivonia Trial, in which he and seven other ANC members were found guilty of a series of charges related to sabotage. Narrowly escaping the death penalty, Mandela was sentenced to life in prison on June 12, 1964. He did not see freedom again for twenty-seven years. When he was released on February 11, 1990, he went on to lead the transitional government and became the first democratically elected president of South Africa, serving just one term, from 1994 to 1999.

What enthralled me most about the autobiography was the section called "The Dark Years." The section's title refers to the

1. Mandela claims he uttered these words during a meeting he called with various local and foreign members of the press after the three-day workers' stay-away had been crushed in May 1961. See Nelson Mandela, *Long Walk to Freedom* (Boston: Little, Brown, 1994), 270. He says something similar during his first televised interview, which he gave to the British television network ITN around the same time. http://www.theatlantic.com/international/archive/2013/12/nelson-mandelas-first-tv-interview-may-1961/282120/.

years Mandela spent imprisoned on Robben Island. It reads like a training manual for surviving dark times. Madiba describes the various hardships imposed at the newly designed prison: a discriminatory dress code and segregated diet that the government created for each of the four racial classes that they had invented, brutal forced labor at the island's lime quarry, and harsh restrictions on visitors and letters (one visitor and one letter were permitted every six months, always censored, often denied altogether). There is a sparse account of Mandela's devastation at the news his mother's death in 1968. This grief was deepened less than a year later when he received a telegram informing him of his eldest son's death as a result of injuries sustained in a car crash. Each of these experiences imposed a distinct psychological pressure: "The challenge for every prisoner, particularly every political prisoner," Mandela counsels, "is how to survive prison intact, how to emerge from prison undiminished, how to conserve and even replenish one's beliefs."[2]

It was not, however, these soul-rending accounts or the leader's startling capacity for perseverance that brought me up short on that long flight. What jolted me awake was, in fact, a dream. Or to be more precise, a nightmare, which Mandela reports returned repeatedly to haunt him during his twenty-seven-year imprisonment:

> I had one recurring nightmare. In the dream, I had just been released from prison—only it was not Robben Island, but a jail in Johannesburg. I walked outside the gates into the city and found no one there to meet me. In fact, there was no one there at all, no people, no cars, no taxis. I would then set out on foot toward Soweto. I walked for many hours before arriving in Orlando West, and then turned the corner toward 8115. Finally, I would

2. Mandela, *Long Walk to Freedom*, 390.

> see my home, but it turned out to be empty, a ghost house, with all
> the doors and windows open, but no one at all there.[3]

I can still remember my sense of astonishment in coming across this passage. It was the middle of the night and I was cramped, reading by that single, sharp light that beams down from the bulkhead. I felt seized by a powerful urge to wake the passenger next to me so I could share the moment with someone. Mandela's nightmare seemed just as dramatic and important as his famous speech from the Rivonia Trial in which he named apartheid's injustice and defined the ideal for which he was prepared to die: a democratic and free society.[4] His nightmare seemed to attest something similarly poignant about his experience of prison, offering both a private account of his emotional state *and* a profound testimony about the political conditions of his unfreedom.

But then came the questions: exactly what kind of statement was this? What does a dream manage to say—or rather *to show*—that is not legible otherwise? Indeed, what does *this* recurring dream manage to show of Mandela's experience of prison? Can this disclosure be understood as a form of political avowal? To what, exactly, does a dream attest? And to whom?

3. Ibid., 496.

4. Excerpts of Mandela's speech are reprinted in his autobiography, and the complete text is available online at http://db.nelsonmandela .org/speeches/pub_view.asp?pg=item&ItemID=NMS010. An audio recording is also available on the *Guardian*'s website: http://www.theguardian .com/world/video/2013/dec/05/nelson-mandela-1964-speech-audio.

Dream-Thinking

AS SIGMUND FREUD TAUGHT US, dreaming is a distinct species of thinking. He wrote voluminously on the subject but offered one of his clearest statements on the matter in a footnote added to *The Interpretation of Dreams* in 1925: "At bottom," he says, "dreams are nothing more than a particular *form* of thinking made possible by the condition of the state of sleep."[1] Dreams *think,* Freud insists, even if this unconscious mode of thought bears little affinity to the more familiar forms of conscious reasoning.

More precisely, Freud proposed that the dreamer *experiences* her thoughts rather than "thinks" them in concepts. Dreams dramatize an idea, constructing a situation out of thoughts that have been transposed into images.[2] And although the particular scenes and actions of dream-life might seem utterly alien to waking thought, they nevertheless arise out of incidents of

1. Sigmund Freud, *The Interpretation of Dreams, Standard Edition* 4 (1900): 506n2. Freud makes a similar point in "Remarks on the Theory and Practice of Dream-Interpretation," *Standard Edition* 19 (1923): 112; "History of the Psychoanalytic Movement," *Standard Edition* 14 (1914): 65; and "Some Neurotic Mechanisms," *Standard Edition* 17 (1922): 229.

2. Freud, *Interpretation of Dreams,* 48–50.

our lived experience. Dream-life is anchored in the material world, tethered to the particular conflicts and conditions of the dreamer's social situation. These thought-events are a "science of the concrete," to borrow Claude Lévi-Strauss's term, a kind of mental bricolage: a particular form of thinking that reuses and recombines bits and pieces of material from the dreamer's diurnal perceptions and the vast storehouse of memory traces.[3]

The various locations mentioned in Mandela's dream can certainly be traced back to sites of his lived experience: the jail in Johannesburg where he spent time as an awaiting-trial prisoner in 1962, prior to the Rivonia Trial, but also the first home he owned, the little red brick house, number 8115 in Orlando West, a place Mandela once called the "center point" of his world, "the place marked with an X in my mental geography."[4] This modest building has subsequently taken on another layer of significance since, in 1999, it was rebuilt and transformed into a museum that now receives thousands of visitors each year. The nightmare also manages to index the tiny cell on Robben Island in which Mandela spent the majority of his sentence, albeit only through a negation: the dream-prison "was *not* Robben Island," he insists. Such cancellations are a telltale sign of repression, a signal that something is being withheld from consciousness because of the pain that would come with its acknowledgment.[5]

3. Claude Lévi-Strauss, "The Science of the Concrete," in *The Savage Mind,* trans. George Weidenfeld, 1–33 (London: Weidenfeld and Nicholson, 1966).

4. Mandela, *Long Walk to Freedom,* 570.

5. Reading psychoanalytically, negative statements are generally understood as taking cognizance of what is repressed. In his 1925 paper called "Negation," Freud writes, "With the help of the symbol of negation, thinking frees itself from the restrictions of repression." Sigmund Freud, "Negation," *Standard Edition* 19 (1925): 239.

While dream-life relies on elements of the dreamer's store-house of experience to weave its landscapes, this is undoubtedly a queer kind of thinking. These uncanny mental events share more than a passing affinity to Franz Kafka's breathtaking thought-landscapes: "When Gregor Samsa woke one morning from uneasy dreams, he found himself transformed into some kind of monstrous vermin."[6] The dream landscape, like Kafka's stories, operates under an unusual set of environmental conditions. Dream-life is not a documentary presentation of events but rather a *symbolic* account of the dreamer's lived experience. In Mandela's case, his dream visually staged the sense of alienation and unfreedom that the prolonged incarceration inflicted: freedom to wander in an empty, uninhabited world is, of course, no freedom at all. Far from being a straightforward fantasy of escape, the nightmare achingly dramatized what a life separated from one's loved ones felt like for the dreamer. It also testified to the experience of being ostracized from the larger political community of humanity, *showing* what it means to be denied that primary dimension of the human condition that involves belonging to a shared gaze—*to see* and *to be seen to exist*.[7]

In Freud's time, just as now, the idea of treating dream-life as an object of study—as a particular *form* of thinking—was considered an outrageous leap. As Freud points out in the opening pages of his *Interpretation of Dreams,* the perplexity this nocturnal phenomenon presented to scientific reasoning is so generally admitted in the literature that "it seems unnecessary

6. Franz Kafka, "The Metamorphosis," in *The Metamorphosis and Other Stories,* trans. Joyce Crick (Oxford: Oxford University Press, 2009), 29.

7. For a discussion of humanity and the gaze, see Hélène Cixous's "Volleys of Humanity," in *Volleys of Humanity: Essays from 1972–2009,* 264–85 (Edinburgh: Edinburgh University Press, 2011).

to quote instances in support of it."[8] Freud's theory of interpretation posed a direct challenge to the logic of the sciences of his day. (This challenge remains just as potent today, in our own era, which is dominated by cognitive models of brain functioning.) By insisting that these seemingly nonsensical psychological events contain meaning and, moreover, that their strange logic is a deliberate attempt to thwart rationality, Freud generated a powerful critique of Enlightenment reasoning.[9] In wrestling with the force of the unconscious, he dared to stray beyond the borders of rational thought and yet refused to jettison meaning from this territory. Or as Jacqueline Rose has more elegantly phrased it, "psychoanalysis starts from the premise that we are freighted with a form of knowledge we cannot bear."[10] Dream-life is one of the key points of contact with this unconscious knowledge that each of us carries but does not quite possess.

Freud was not alone in his exploration of the territory that lies beyond the gates of rationality. In the latter half of the twentieth century, a variety of political thinkers began to notice the cracks in the bedrock of reason that had once served as the privileged foundation of political thought. Some of these theorists diagnosed the Enlightenment itself as a disturbed form of thinking and began searching for alternatives. In the preface to her collection of essays *Between Past and Future,* Hannah Arendt offers a terse account of this landscape of postwar critique. Having barely escaped the Nazis' genocidal de-

8. Freud, *Interpretation of Dreams,* 1.

9. For more on psychoanalysis as a critique of scientific reason, see Léon Chertok and Isabelle Stengers, *A Critique of Psychoanalytic Reason: Hypnosis as a Scientific Problem from Lavoisier to Lacan,* trans. Martha Noel Evans (Stanford, Calif.: Stanford University Press, 1992).

10. Jacqueline Rose, "Review of *What Is Madness* by Darian Leader," *Guardian,* October 1, 2011.

signs, Arendt knew all too well how political terror could be unleashed in the voice of reason. She notes that the French intellectuals who joined the *résistance* and who founded existentialism were not the first, nor the last, to have "outbursts of passionate exasperation with reason, thought, and rational discourse." Such are "the natural reactions of men who know from their own experiences that thought and reality have parted company."[11] But in her characteristically strong-minded way, Arendt dismissed existentialism as representing little more than a form of escapism—an attempt to evade the dilemmas of dark times by retreating into an "unquestioning commitment to action."[12] In her mind, becoming an *engagée* was no solution for the profound problems that arise when reason breaks with reality.

For the latter half of her life, Arendt searched for an elastic form of thinking that could endure the dilemmas of dark times. She wrote at length about the problem of "thoughtlessness," and yet she never gave up on the activity of thinking. The essays that make up her collection *Between Past and Future* represent a series of such experiments in thinking otherwise. She subtitled the collection "Eight Exercises in Political Thought." They are not prescriptions about *what* to think so much as experiments in *how* to think. Like many theorists of her generation, Arendt moved away from sweeping philosophical treatises and opted

11. Hannah Arendt, *Between Past and Future: Eight Exercises in Political Thought* (New York: Penguin 1968), 6. The Frankfurt School's absence in Arendt's narrative is noticeable. As Elizabeth Young-Bruehl has documented, Arendt carried a lifelong antipathy toward the Frankfurt Institute and toward Theodor Adorno in particular. See Young-Bruehl's *Hannah Arendt: For the Love of the World,* 2nd ed. (New Haven, Conn.: Yale University Press, 2004), 80, 109, and 166–67, respectively.

12. Arendt, *Between Past and Future,* 8.

instead to examine aspects of our shared intellectual tradition from the standpoint of subjective experience. She advocated for a kind of thinking that arose out of the "actuality of political incidents." Her assumption was that "thought itself arises out of incidents of living experience and must remain bound to them as the only guideposts by which to take its bearings."[13]

Mandela can be taken as an exemplar of such thinking. Over and over, Madiba demonstrated the kind of "enlarged thought" that the political theorist championed. Arendt borrowed this term from Immanuel Kant (she worked closely with the philosopher's theory of judgment in her late lectures "Kant's Political Philosophy"[14]). For both thinkers, "enlarged thought" is an exemplary mental process by which one imagines the world from the perspective of the other, or, as Kant articulated it, "to think from the standpoint of everyone else."[15] The philosopher situated this activity as one of the maxims for a common human understanding, and Arendt extended this line of thinking to argue that this specific mental process was integral to our collective political reality—an indispensable exercise of imagination that actually creates and sustains our common public world.

When the "hope of Africa" sprang through prison's door in 1994, not only was his "stupendous heart" and "gargantuan will" intact but Mandela had also somehow managed to use his twenty-seven years of imprisonment to grow his capacity

13. Ibid., 14.

14. Hannah Arendt, *Lectures on Kant's Political Philosophy,* ed. Ronald Beiner (Chicago: University of Chicago Press, 1992).

15. Immanuel Kant, *The Critique of Judgment,* trans. James Creed Meredith (Oxford: Oxford University Press, 1957), 152. The other two maxims include the ability to think for oneself and the ability to think consistently.

to think from the standpoint of others.[16] When he took the seat of presidency in a country in which he had previously not been allowed to vote, he personally—and courteously—invited his former prison guards to sit in the front rows of his inauguration. As Rita Barnard has argued, Mandela's approach to politics borrowed from the genre of the sublime, which is to say, his expansive understanding of freedom exceeded the confines of all the available models that traditionally give shape to this ideal.[17] South Africa's transition to democracy certainly cannot be attributed to one man—and Mandela's record is not without controversy—but there can be no doubt that his striking capacity to think from the standpoint of others had an integral part to play in the larger transformation of his country. Mandela's example underscores Arendt's fundamental insight: that the individual's ability *to think* has a profound relationship to the political commons.

Mandela himself provides a brief account of how he came to acquire this enlarged mentality in the closing paragraphs of his autobiography: "I was not born with a hunger to be free," he writes, although as a boy he felt free—free to run in the fields, swim in the streams, roast mealies, and ride the broad backs of the bulls in his village. It was only as a young man that he began to understand that his boyhood freedom was an illusion, and it was then that his gnawing hunger began. As a student, and then as a barrister in Johannesburg, he yearned for the freedom not to be obstructed in earning a living wage, to marry and raise a family, to live a lawful life. But he found that achieving these goals did not satisfy his hunger: "I saw that it was not just my

16. Maya Angelou, "His Day Is Done," in *The Complete Poetry* (New York: Random House, 2015), 306.
17. See Rita Barnard's introduction to *The Cambridge Companion to Nelson Mandela* (New York: Cambridge University Press, 2014), 3.

freedom that was curtailed, but the freedom of everyone who looked like I did." Joining the ANC helped him understand that his hunger was indivisible from the freedom of his people to live with dignity: "the chains on any one of my people were the chains on all of them, the chains on all of my people were the chains on me."

Such narratives of disillusionment are familiar enough as the makings of a freedom fighter. But Mandela's thought had more maturing to do. The long and lonely years in prison transformed his hunger for his people's freedom into a hunger for the freedom of all people:

> I knew as well as I knew anything that the oppressor must be liberated just as surely as the oppressed. A man who takes away another man's freedom is a prisoner of hatred, he is locked behind the bars of prejudice and narrow-mindedness. . . . The oppressed and the oppressor alike are robbed of their humanity.
>
> When I walked out of prison, that was my mission, to liberate the oppressed and the oppressor both. Some say that has now been achieved. But I know that is not the case. The truth is that we are not yet free; we have merely achieved the freedom to be free, the right not to be oppressed. We have not taken the final step of our journey, but the first step on a longer and even more difficult road. For to be free is not merely to cast off one's chains, but to live in a way that respects and enhances the freedom of others.[18]

In these stirring closing passages, one can hear echoes of a universal humanism that stretches from the eighteenth-century revolutions through to the United Nations's Declaration of Human Rights. There are also deep reverberations that come from years of anticolonial struggle and the wellspring of *ubuntu,* an African-

18. Mandela, *Long Walk to Freedom,* 624–25.

born philosophy that attends to the obligations of kinship and advocates a model of humanity-in-reciprocity: the profound sense that we are human only through the humanity of others. Mandela's ability to borrow from a startlingly wide range of political traditions makes him one of the exemplars of enlarged thought. He gave birth to an indivisible notion of freedom, which, aside from transforming him into a global icon for human rights, can serve as a model for Arendt's signature claim that "the *raison d'être* of politics is freedom."[19]

I am aware that I have taken us on a detour away from the particulars of Mandela's nightmare. The point of this diversion was not only to make a case for Madiba's significance as an exemplary political thinker of the twentieth century but also to show that some of the most potent and transformative forms of political thought do not depend on rationality. In dark times, another form of thinking is needed.

Mandela's dream bears the scars of such a climate. A recurring nightmare is a particular form of thinking that operates under the pressure of fear. The dreams that leave us crying out in the dark demand a special kind of psychological work. In Wilfred Bion's terms, these frightening mental events are the psyche's attempt to digest a particularly difficult emotional experience. The dream subjects the dreamer's emotional pain to a specific form of unconscious work that is designed to issue in psychological growth.[20]

Put more simply, nightmares call for courage. And as Hannah Arendt noted, courage is cardinal among the political virtues.[21] This attribute is what enables and emboldens us to leave the

19. Arendt, *Between Past and Future,* 146.

20. Wilfred Bion, *Learning from Experience* (London: Karnac, 1962), 8.

21. Arendt, *Between Past and Future,* 156.

protective confines of our homes and to enter the public realm. Mandela's example reminds us that courage does not come without its share of anguish. The recurring nightmare is one example of its psychic cost, but Madiba's autobiography is filled with descriptions of the excruciating divide that he felt between the obligations of family life and the obligations of public life. (In the closing pages, one can find the final wrenching account: "It was as simple and yet as incomprehensible as the moment when a small child asks her father, 'Why can you not be with us?' And the father must utter the terrible words, 'There are other children like you, a great many of them . . .' and then one's voice trails off."[22]) Mandela spent the better part of his lifetime digesting this difficult knowledge: in dark times, it is not only individual lives at stake but the larger human world.

From this fraught climate, the significance of dream-life can perhaps begin to stand out. To transpose Arendt's terms into a Freudian key: dreaming is an integral exercise of thought, an alternative landscape built out of incidents of living experience and a prime model of our fundamental human capacity to assign meaning to the world. Without relying on the banisters of existent concepts, dream-thinking manages to dramatize and metabolize our most profound conflicts, geolocating the moorings of our subjectivity within the gossamer web of social relations, all without losing an inch in the riches, varieties, and dramatic elements that are so characteristic of "real" life.

The chapters that follow elaborate this central premise, echoing and deepening the idea that dream-thinking is integral to the political realm. Each of the chapters pursues an interrelated idea: (1) dream-work as a model of civil defense, (2) narrating a dream as a discourse that acts, and (3) dreaming as a practice of freedom.

22. Mandela, *Long Walk to Freedom,* 623.

The guiding principle that animates these explorations is borrowed from the pediatrician and psychoanalyst D. W. Winnicott, who, at the close of the Second World War, offered this wise counsel: "Thinking is but a snare and a delusion unless the unconscious is taken into account."[23]

23. D. W. Winnicott, "Thinking and the Unconscious," *The Liberal Magazine*, March 1945, repr. in *Home Is Where We Start From* (New York: W. W. Norton, 1990), 169.

Dream-Work as Civil Defense

ONE OF THE THINGS that makes dreams infinitely more adventurous, more inventive, and more cunning than daytime thought is the fact that this thought-landscape is not governed by the rules of rationality but rather relies on an alternative mode of mental functioning in which meaning moves more freely. Dreaming is just one example of unconscious thinking, but it was through the extended examination and interpretation of these oneiric events that Freud discovered the structure of this "other" psychological agency.

In *The Interpretation of Dreams,* Freud distinguished between two separate functions that occur in the formation of a dream, both of which operate unconsciously: (1) the production of the *dream-thoughts* and (2) the transformation of these thoughts into the manifest content of the dream through the operations of the *dream-work*.[1]

Dream-thoughts are the dense web of thoughts and ideas that are latent in a dream but that can be gradually unearthed through the dreamer's associations, that is, all the memories, thoughts, and images that each element of the dream brings

1. Freud, *Interpretation of Dreams,* 506.

to mind. For the first half of his career, Freud maintained that these dream-thoughts were arranged according to a pleasure principle, hence his oft-cited thesis that a dream is the fulfillment of a repressed wish. This led some analysts to assume that dreams could be distilled to a single desire, but Freud more often than not described dream-thoughts in terms of a dense thicket, as "a complex of thoughts and memories of the most intricate possible structure, with all the attributes of trains of thought familiar to us in waking life."[2]

For a time, Freud was preoccupied by these intricate "trains of thought," which, as he notes, can emerge from more than one center. But as his thinking matured, he realized that the more radical aspect of dream-life was not the unconscious thoughts themselves but the particular way these thoughts are transformed by the dynamic agency of the *dream-work*. Freud used this latter term as a heading under which he listed four distinct operations of transformation: displacement, condensation, symbolization, and secondary revision.[3] I will not attempt

2. Ibid., 311–12.

3. Readers of Freud will recognize that my terminology does not match what is set out in *Interpretation of Dreams*. Freud himself described the four mechanisms of the dream as *Verdichtung* (condensation), *Verschiebung* (displacement), *Rücksicht auf Darstellbarkeit* (considerations of representability), and *sekundäre Bearbeitung* (secondary revision). He consistently revised these terms, and subsequent analysts have further modified his language. I am leaning in particular here on a particular strand of clinical theory that treats dreaming as an unconscious form of thinking about emotional experience. Here the dream-work is taken as exemplary of a wider concept that is fundamental to contemporary clinical psychoanalysis, namely, psychic work. See Ella Sharpe, *Dream Analysis* (London: Hogarth, 1959); Hanna Segal, "Notes on Symbol Formation," in *The Work of Hanna Segal: A Kleinian Approach to Clinical Practice*, 49–65 (London: Free Association Books, 1986), and Segal, "The Function of Dreams," ibid., 89–97; Segal, *Dream, Phantasy, and Art*

to explain each of these complex operations here, but it is important to emphasize the distinction between the dream-work and the dream-thoughts. The dream-work does not generate the dream's content but rather works to transfigure it. Dream-work is a *treatment* of experience, in the artistic or chemical sense of the term, a kind of metamorphosis, which, Freud realized, is one of our primary means to give meaning to experience, indeed, an archetype for the freedom of thought. The dream-work, as he put it, "restricts itself to giving things a new form," and he regularly insisted that "the essence" of dreaming is this psychological work of reformulation.[4] In other words, Freud came to realize that the most radical aspect of dream-life was not *what* these experiences think but *how* they think.

The significance of this distinction is readily evident in Mandela's nightmare. As the dreamer himself admits, the nightmare arose from a desperate wish to return home to see his family. This hardly seems surprising for someone facing lifetime imprisonment. Where the dream draws its poignancy and its potency is in *how* it negotiates this desire, *how* it drama-

---

(London: Routledge, 1991); W. R. Bion, *Learning from Experience* (London: Karnac, 1962); J.-B. Pontalis, *Frontiers in Psychoanalysis: Between the Dream and Psychic Pain,* trans. Catherine Cullen and Philip Cullen (London: Hogarth Press, 1981); Donald Meltzer, *Dream-Life: A Re-examination of the Psycho-analytical Theory and Technique* (Oxford: Clunie Press, 1984); Thomas Ogden, *This Art of Psychoanalysis: Dreaming Undreamt Dreams and Interrupted Cries* (London: Karnac, 2005); and Christopher Bollas, "The Wisdom of the Dream," in *The Christopher Bollas Reader,* 249–58 (London: Routledge, 2011).

4. Freud, *Interpretation of Dreams,* 507. In his 1923 paper "Remarks on the Theory and Practice of Dream Interpretation," Freud also warns analysts against the lure of trying to uncover the latent content at the expense of attending to the dream-work, the particular formal transformations that the dream performs. Sigmund Freud, "Remarks on the Theory and Practice of Dream Interpretation," *Standard Edition* 19 (1923): 112.

tizes the experience of being severed from contact with human society. This severing was particularly extreme in the first few years of Mandela's prison sentence—when he was only allowed to receive one visitor and one letter every six months—but the process of his political isolation began long before his actual incarceration. In 1952, the future president was among a group of leaders who were banned by the Afrikaner government through its Suppression of Communism Act. Although this act specifically targeted Communists, it was worded broadly so as to include "any activity that allegedly promoted social, political, or economic change in South Africa." The banning aimed, in the short term, to prevent a variety of political figures from attending the national conferences of their respective parties. It was the first of a long series of bans that Mandela faced in the decade prior to his imprisonment.

Being banned in apartheid South Africa meant one's movements were severely restricted. Mandela was rarely allowed to leave his district of Johannesburg. It also prevented him from attending meetings of all kinds, not just political ones. He was prohibited, for instance, from attending his children's birthday parties or from speaking to more than one person at a time (both of which he defied the law to do). Banning was a kind of "walking imprisonment," and the strategy was one of the government's systematic attempts to immobilize leaders of groups who were resisting apartheid.[5] Whereas a government banning a particular political organization is a common enough practice, the National Party's policy of banning *individuals* was something unique among modern nations. Not since the Middle Ages had a government openly attempted to formalize this kind

5. Mandela, *Long Walk to Freedom,* 135.

of juridical outlawry.[6] Apart from physical restrictions, banned persons were forced to resign any offices they held in any organization, and they were prohibited from speaking publicly or from writing for any publication. A banned person could not be quoted publicly, and his photograph was prohibited from being circulated. Shortly before Mandela was due to be released in 1990, *Time* magazine produced an illustrated portrait of the leader on its cover because no photographs of the freedom fighter were available. No one knew what the man looked like after twenty-seven years of imprisonment.

The example tests the outer edges of what Jenny Edkins calls "face politics."[7] Banned individuals were denied legal safeguards in the event of disappearance or death. In effect, banning represented an organized political attempt to expunge a person from all aspects of social and public life, a gesture that sought to render an individual into a kind of *homo sacer*—an accursed figure who is deprived of the usual entitlements and protections of human society. Mandela himself described this political act as an impingement of spirit: "Banning not only confines one physically, it imprisons one's spirit. It induces a kind of psychological claustrophobia that makes one yearn not only for freedom of movement but spiritual escape."[8]

Theorists such as Giorgio Agamben, Jacques Derrida, and others have analyzed the structural force of this kind of sovereign violence to great effect, but Mandela's dream offers a

---

6. Of course, totalitarian governments have always found various ways to "disappear" individuals and groups deemed undesirable, whether through purification laws (such as the racial policies in Nazi Germany) or individually targeted political exile (such as Madame Germaine de Staël's banishment from France during Napoleon's reign).

7. Jenny Edkins, *Face Politics* (London: Routledge, 2015).

8. Mandela, *Long Walk to Freedom*, 144.

rather different site through which to consider its lived experience.[9] My phrasing here is deliberate: "lived experience" is a translation of the German neologism *Erlebnis,* which has been the subject of a long-standing philosophical debate. The term was coined in an effort to distinguish a particular category of experience that is distinct from the common use of this term *(Erfahrung).* In contrast to the usual sense of experience, *Erlebnis* refers to a kind of intensified experience, one that is rooted in feeling rather than an objective or otherwise detached rendering of the event. Mandela's nightmare, in this respect, offers a direct account of the experience of being banned without recourse to an empirical or philosophical description of this condition: the dream directly expresses the emotional experience of having one's very personhood scraped away. All dreams are individual accounts of lived experience in this respect—graphic re-presentations that allow for a more intimate grappling with one's condition.

For the philosophers, lived experience is properly understood as a category of consciousness.[10] Dreams, however, are a

9. See Giorgio Agamben, *Homo Sacer: Sovereign Power and Bare Life,* trans. Daniel Heller-Roazen (Stanford, Calif.: Stanford University Press, 1998); Jacques Derrida, "The Force of Law: 'The Mystical Foundation of Authority,'" *Cardozo Law Review* 11 (1990): 920–1046; Derrida, *The Beast and the Sovereign,* 2 vols., ed. Michel Lisse, Marie-Louise Mallet, and Ginette Michaud, trans. Geoffrey Bennington (Chicago: University of Chicago Press, 2009–2011).

10. In *Truth and Method,* Hans-Georg Gadamer outlines how the noun *Erlebnis,* in the first instance, means "to be alive when something happens" and thus speaks to the sense of proximity and immediacy—something that one has experienced for oneself. But the form *das Erlebte* also refers to a sense of sustained insight that is achieved as a result of the immediate experience: "Something becomes an 'experience' not only insofar as it is experienced, but insofar as its being experienced makes a special impression that gives it lasting importance." *Erlebnis,* therefore,

decidedly unconscious form of thinking. The material that composes the landscape of dream-life is often derived from those aspects of experience that the dreamer has either repressed or not yet emotionally processed. Indeed, part of the dream's aim is to bring to consciousness this "unthought known," to metabolize the experience in a way that makes it available as a form of emotional understanding.[11] Put differently, dream-thinking works to transform objective occurrences into subjective phenomena. Mandela's nightmare allowed him to articulate and to work through the emotional impact of his juridical sentence, rendering its impact in his own terms. This is one of our most intimate venues to exercise the freedom of expression.

The agency that performs this transformative labor is the dream-work. More specifically, Mandela's nightmare relied on *symbolization* to articulate the emotional significance of his experience of being erased from society. Symbolization (or what Freud initially named "considerations of representability") renders experience figuratively—presenting an idea or an emotion in pictorial terms. In the nightmare, Johannesburg was devoid of all people, all cars, and Mandela's home was turned into a ghost house. This empty landscape serves as a dramatic figure

---

refers to a kind of defining moment, an exceptional experience that is nevertheless tied to the everyday, which, in turn, is folded back to fertilize a larger, historical understanding of a life. Phenomenologists privilege this category of lived experience because it captures a sense of immediacy that precedes the more rationalized processes of description. See Gadamer, *Truth and Method,* trans. Joel Weinsheimer and Donald G. Marshall (London: Bloomsbury, 2004), 55–56.

11. Christopher Bollas's term, the "unthought known," refers to unconscious knowledge that is not emotionally digested enough to be able to be consciously "thought." See Bollas, *The Shadow of the Object: Psychoanalysis and the Unthought Known* (New York: Columbia University Press, 1987).

of the emotional experience of being banished. Mandela's experience of being barred from society, and of spending a great portion of his life imprisoned, felt akin to a world emptied of all human presence. In this respect, the nightmare gave form to the violence that imprisonment enacts, and more specifically, the violence that apartheid enacts: it figuratively conveyed the pain of depriving a human being access to the human world. For those it targets, apartheid transforms the world into a ghost town.

In more intimate terms, the dream-work's symbolic elaborations serve as a protective shield against attacks on our being—whether biological or psychological traumas or social and political forms of aggression. As Arendt helps us to understand, political violence does not simply target the body of its subjects; it aims to destroy the subject's capacity to think. Political violence attacks the mental life of the citizenry. The dream-work's transfigurations attempt to work through these forms of aggression. The symbolic elaborations aim to preserve our mental agency, in part by generating what Didier Anzieu describes as a "psychic envelope," a secondary, protective skin for thought.[12] Mandela's recurring dream opened an interior landscape in which he had space *to think* about the terms of his political condition rather than be directly *equated* with it. The opera-

12. Didier Anzieu, *The Skin Ego: A Psychoanalytic Approach to Self*, trans. Chris Turner (New Haven, Conn.: Yale University Press, 1989). As mentioned earlier, I am condensing a particular strand of psychoanalytic theory that has theorized dream-work as a process of thinking that is akin to "working through." This approach modifies Freud's thinking about symbolization. Whereas Freud had a somewhat rigid sense of symbol formation—he imagined a constancy of the relationship between the symbol and what it represents—later analysts emphasize *symbolic function*: what the particular *use* of the symbol allows in terms of psychological development.

tions of dream-work helped shield and sustain his sense of self by enabling him to turn his political condition into a figure of thought. Or to use Mandela's own terms, this alternative mode of thinking helped him defend himself against that dimension of political violence that aimed to imprison his spirit. Dream-life, in this respect, can be understood as a primal form of resistance, indeed, as our most intimate model of civil defense. Freud famously described dreams as the guardians of sleep, but they are much more than that—these night watchmen preserve our psychic functioning, guard over our capacity to think, and, in so doing, shield us against the world's impingements.

A caveat: dreams do not automatically issue in psychological growth. As several clinicians have shown, many psychological events occur in sleep that greatly resemble dreaming but involve no unconscious psychological work; these events possess nothing of the *labor* of dream-thinking. Hanna Segal, for instance, describes patients whose dreams simply serve to evacuate unwanted emotions or ideas.[13] Analysts often distinguish, in this respect, between different degrees of symbol formation. The capacity to form and use symbols depends on one's relationship to unconscious fantasy, which is to say, the degree and nature of the communication that one has with one's internal objects. To cast this in Arendt's terms, one's capacity to think depends on one's willingness to establish a dialogue with oneself. It is a testament to Mandela's great strength of mind that he was able to use the solitude that prison imposed to engage, as he put it, in "conversations with myself."[14]

13. Hannah Segal wrote extensively on the subject of dreaming and symbol formation. Two important papers include "Notes on Symbol Formation," *International Journal of Psychoanalysis* (1957), and "The Function of Dreams," both reprinted in *Work of Hanna Segal.*

14. Mandela, *Conversations with Myself* (New York: Farrar, Straus, and Giroux, 2010).

A Discourse That Acts

ALTHOUGH EASILY OVERLOOKED, the disclosure of any dream relies on a fundamental act of translation: the conversion of the dream that is *dreamed in images* into the dream that is *articulated in words*. Dreaming is first and foremost an experience that takes place on an unconscious plane, usually under the cover of sleep. Narrating a dream is a secondary act of translation that occurs at some later point—presuming that one has managed to smuggle the dream through that delicate border between sleep and awakening.

Freud was attentive to the way dream-thoughts are transformed into verbal expressions. His interpretations tend to focus on the ambiguity of language. In *The Interpretation of Dreams,* he frequently traces the various connotative nodes that issue from a single word in the dream-text.[1] However, it was one of Freud's contemporaries, Sándor Ferenczi, who first drew attention to the larger distinction between the experience of dreaming and the gesture of disclosing this experience to an-

1. Freud elaborated his thoughts about the function of words as a complex presentation that combines auditory, visual, and kinaesthetic elements in Appendix C of "The Unconscious," *Standard Edition* 14 (1915): 209–15.

other person. Ferenczi was a Hungarian analyst in Freud's inner circle, and he became particularly attuned to the way people relayed their dreams. In 1912, he wrote that dreamers often feel impelled to convey their dreams "to the very person to whom the content relates."[2] This observation opened the door to a new understanding of dream-life as a special kind of communication *between* subjects. Whereas the activity of dreaming is a dialogue that one has with oneself, in the disclosure of this experience, a dream becomes a form of communication with another person—an unconscious avowal that involves both a sender and an addressee. In this way, reporting a dream is simultaneously a kind of publication of the dream-work and an action that moves the dream into another venue. Here dreaming becomes a speech act.

In clinical terms, dreaming represents an *intra*-psychic form of dialogue that takes place within the realm of the "dream-space," whereas the narration of a dream represents an *inter*-subjective form of communication that occurs between the dreamer and her interlocutor.[3] Contemporary clinicians are particularly attuned to the way patients communicate their dreams to the analyst. They take note, for instance, of the difference between a patient who reluctantly reports "I had a dream last night but only scraps of it are left . . ." and a patient who eagerly expounds upon every detail of the previous night's adventures. The style in which one communicates a dream indi-

2. See Sándor Ferenczi, "To Whom Does One Relate One's Dream?" (1912), reprinted in *Further Contributions to the Theory and Technique of Psycho-analysis,* 349 (London: Hogarth Press, 1950), and Ferenczi, "Dreams of the Unsuspecting" (1916–17), reprinted ibid., 346–48.

3. Masud Khan, "The Use and Abuse of Dream in Psychic Experience" (1972), reprinted in *The Privacy of the Self,* 306–15 (New York: International Universities Press, 1974).

cates a variety of things, including the relationship the dreamer has with her own dream-thinking, which is conveyed in the particular way she gives this object over to a third party for examination—or, conversely, the way she withholds it.[4]

Not surprisingly, debate has ensued about the significance of this distinction between the act of dreaming and reporting the experience to another person. Is dreaming an experience that is designed to protect the privacy of the self? What, exactly, is being disclosed when one conveys a dream? How can reporting one's dream expose or perhaps even betray the self? Freud grappled with some of these questions early on. In the preface to the first edition of *The Interpretation of Dreams,* he explicitly asked his readers to grant him "the right of freedom of thought—in my dream-life, if nowhere else."[5] The entreaty refers to the fact that Freud had used his own dreams (as well as those of his patients) as the key source material for the book. This put him in something of a tight spot. As he acknowledges, "it inevitably followed that I should have to reveal to the public gaze more of the intimacies of my mental life than I liked, or than is normally necessary for any writer who is a man of science and not a poet." Here Freud is defending his unusual method and his unorthodox data. The preface closes with the plea to his readers to accept this situation and that if anyone finds any sort of reference to himself in the book, "grant me the right of freedom of thought—in my dream-life, if nowhere else."

Freud's concerns about public exposure spawn further questions when the dream under scrutiny belongs to the world's most famous political prisoner: what does it mean for Mandela to reveal the intimacies of his mental life to the public gaze?

---

4. Pontalis, *Frontiers in Psychoanalysis,* 28.
5. Freud, *Interpretation of Dreams,* xxiiv.

What does dream-life have to do with his capacity for the freedom of thought? And what does the freedom of thought have to do with the freedom of speech? What does it mean to *speak* of freedom? And how does one come to be free to speak of it?

These fundamental questions about the relationship between dreaming and freedom have a particular vector in the psychoanalytic clinic. In a trilogy of papers published between 1962 and 1976, the British-based psychoanalyst Masud Khan sought to find ways to return the experience of dreaming to the dreamer.[6] Khan came to believe that the role of the analyst should primarily be to help establish and support the patient's dreaming capacity, that is, to help patients gain more freedom in their symbolic functioning. Drawing from his clinical practice, Khan argued that patients who were unable to establish and effectively use the dream-space tended to exploit external reality as a venue to act out their unconscious conflicts and fantasies. A dream that enables an "actualization *in* the dream-space," Khan proposed, curtails "acting out in social-space."[7] By the end of his career, Khan had begun to view the distinction between the dreaming experience and the disclosure of a dream as a decisive one. In his last paper on the subject, he went so far as to describe the communication of the dream as a negation of the experience of dreaming: "Dreaming itself," he declared, "is beyond interpretation."[8]

6. Masud Khan, "Dream Psychology and the Evolution of the Psychoanalytic Situation" (1962), reprinted in *Privacy of the Self,* 27–41; Khan, "The Use and Abuse of Dream in Psychic Experience" (1972), reprinted ibid., 306–15; and Khan, "The Changing Use of Dreams in Psychoanalytic Practice," *International Journal of Psychoanalysis* 57 (1976): 325–30.

7. Khan, "Use and Abuse of Dream," 314.

8. Khan, "Changing Use of Dreams," 328.

Khan's close colleague, the French analyst J.-B. Pontalis, echoed some of these concerns and strongly disagreed with others. Pontalis admitted, "In a sense, psychoanalysis strangles the eloquence of dream life."[9] But he took issue with Khan's move to privilege the dream experience at the expense of communicating the dream. Pontalis felt that attempts to cloister dream-life in the private, inner domain of the self deprive this experience of its primary function: *to bring conflicts to the surface.* For Pontalis, the act of interpretation is undoubtedly a symbolic wound to the privacy of the dreaming experience, but a wound that works in tandem with the dream-work's own procedures of substitution and transformation. Psychoanalysis, Pontalis emphasized, is a talking cure—a form of treatment that rests on the principle that the ability to freely speak to another person is integral to the relief of psychic pain.

In a more general sense, almost every parent knows that getting a child to relay a nightmare helps to lessen some of its hallucinatory force. Relief arrives precisely because the dream that is captured in words is something different from the dream as experienced. Translating and transmitting the experience of a nightmare help to absorb the shock of the event. As Pontalis puts it, "the power of speech answers the imaginary power of the dream and takes its place."[10]

Dream-life becomes most *politically* potent in its verbal disclosure. Mandela reported his recurring nightmare in the context of his autobiography and, in so doing, aimed to establish a particular kind of relationship with his readers. (He sent a different iteration of this dream to his wife, Winnie, in a 1976 letter—a gesture that intended to establish a rather differ-

9. Pontalis, *Frontiers in Psychoanalysis,* 33.
10. Ibid., 37.

ent kind of relationship.[11]) Language is, of course, a system of communication, but it is also an agency—an act that has consequences. Many verbal statements are designed simply to convey information, but as J. L. Austin taught us, some utterances have more concrete effects: a royal decree, a judge's ruling, an assessor's appraisal.[12] In each of these cases, the speaker uses language as an agency, as a means to perform an action.

As a lawyer and a banned figure, Mandela was well attuned to the performative power of language—and the language of law in particular. Indeed, this intimacy was significant to his political practice. Early on in the freedom fighter's career, Madiba helped organize a wide-scale resistance movement that took aim at the Afrikaner government's institution of apartheid laws, the Population Registration Act and the Group Areas Act chief among them. These laws stripped people of their rights under the guise of preserving them. The ANC's Defiance Campaign staged demonstrations in which volunteers strategically defied some of these new laws: marching through restricted areas without permits, entering railway stations through the "Europeans Only" entrance, and sitting on benches marked "Vir Blankes" ("For Whites"). The Defiance Campaign necessarily defined human beings as subjects-of-law, that is, as citizens who were being subjected to unfair apartheid policies. Because these laws positioned subjects in unequal ways in relation to the state, a vital part of the liberation struggle involved actively resisting these forms of subjugation.

The political principle behind the Defiance Campaign involves denying the sovereign authority of apartheid laws and creating instead, as Mandela put it, "conditions which will

11. Mandela, *Long Walk to Freedom,* 496–97.

12. J. L. Austin, *How to Do Things with Words* (Cambridge, Mass.: Harvard University Press, 1962).

restore human dignity, equality and freedom to every South African."[13] The principle of defying an unjust law lies at the heart of civil disobedience. But from where does the restoration of dignity arrive? From what sovereignty will the disenfranchised claim their franchise, if not from the law? The ANC's implicit answer (borrowed from Gandhi's example) is that the indivisible freedom of every South African is held *as a thought* in the gesture of defiance itself, even if the resources of liberation are not yet available. One might say that such gestures receive their authority from a freedom that is not present but whose existence is nevertheless indexed by the gesture. As the philosopher Jean-Luc Nancy suggests, "the thinking of freedom can only be seized, surprised, and taken from elsewhere by the very thing it thinks."[14]

Mandela's nightmare also demonstrates this characteristic "thinking of freedom." The disclosure exhibits the mechanics of the performative act that lies at the heart of this political wager—the elsewhere from which freedom springs. By its nature, dreaming carries us beyond the borders of the sovereign ego. Indeed, a nightmare is one of the more intimate experiences of being subjected to a foreign agency. This is precisely what makes these events so unsettling: the frightening images and sensations that arrive under the cover of sleep are not within the dreamer's command but rather arrive unbidden.

Disclosing this experience has a dual performative effect: first, the imaginary operations of the dream-work free up the linguistic structures that traditionally govern our capacity as

13. From the address Nelson Mandela made to the ANC (Transvaal) Congress, September 21, 1953. Available online at http://www.mandela.gov.za/mandela_speeches/.

14. Jean-Luc Nancy, *The Experience of Freedom,* trans. Bridget McDonald (Stanford, Calif.: Stanford University Press, 1993), 8.

speaking beings—dreams enable and provoke us to say things that we might feel otherwise unable to say. In this respect, the dream-work's re-formative power liberates the inhibitions and constraints of rational thought and speech—constraints that are particularly profound in dark times. The activity of dreaming is an exercise of the freedom of thought, and the disclosure of a dream *enacts* the freedom of speech.

Second, reporting a dream is an avowal of the dreaming experience. By disclosing his nightmare, Mandela testified to his lived experience; he affirmed *whom* he was by placing himself in a particular relationship to his readers. Speaking with a view to freedom anchors the speaker within the web of human relations. The gesture establishes the structure of the relationship between subjects and sets the terms of political exchange. The intimate nature of Mandela's disclosure is signal in this respect. In 1994, the same year he was elected president, he made a list in one of his notebooks; the first item: "Personalize political experience."[15]

Our common world is borne on the backs of political actors who demonstrate the courage to disclose themselves to one another. By sharing his dream-life, Mandela reaffirmed this fundamental fact: the public sphere is created and sustained through such exercises of freedom.

15. Mandela, *Conversations with Myself,* 350.

Dreaming as a Practice
of Freedom

ALTHOUGH PROMOTED AS AN AUTOBIOGRAPHY, *Long Walk to Freedom* was in large part the work of a collective. The original manuscript was begun clandestinely in 1974, while Mandela was still imprisoned on Robben Island. He describes writing deep into the night and in the morning passing off finished sections to a handful of comrades who would add comments in the margins. Ahmed Kathrada, Mandela's longtime friend and fellow prisoner, describes "an editorial board" of trusted ANC members who worked collectively on the original draft, which was then transcribed into microscopic print and smuggled off the island in 1976. Then in the 1990s, after Mandela's release, the manuscript was adapted once again by an American journalist, Richard Stengel, with Kathrada and other advisors forming yet another collective to oversee the final editing process.[1] Although the narrative is written in first person, the Nelson Mandela we encounter in the autobiography is very much a *persona* in the ancient sense—a mask worn by a dramatic character in a play.

1. Verne Harris, introduction to Mandela, *Conversations with Myself,* xv.

In this respect, *Long Walk to Freedom* belongs to the genre of what Philip Holden calls "national autobiography." These narratives work to ally the life of a leader with the process of decolonization. Other examples include Gandhi's *The Story of My Experiments with Truth* and Lee Kuan Yew's *The Singapore Story*.[2] This particular variation on the bildungsroman helps shape the new nation using the material of an imagined individual rather than an "imagined community," as Benedict Anderson famously proposed. The exemplary figure provides a model for the citizen to identify with and an example to follow. And for the newly democratic South Africa, this imagined individual was Nelson Mandela.

Long Walk to Freedom does not, therefore, belong to the order of Marcus Aurelius's *Meditations* or Augustine's *Confessions*. This autobiography is not a book of personal thoughts, written to oneself. It does not reveal the inner life of the icon, even as it trades on and stimulates the powerful desire to come to know something of Madiba's private struggles. Indeed, as any number of accounts show, Mandela was not introspective about his emotional life. He often became frustrated—and sometimes even angry—when prompted to discuss his feelings.[3]

It might be tempting, in this respect, to cast Mandela's recurring nightmare as a rare glimpse into the great leader's otherwise impenetrable internal world. However, it is more

2. Philip Holden, *Autobiography and Decolonization: Modernity, Masculinity, and the Nation-State* (Madison: University of Wisconsin Press, 2008).

3. Richard Stengel, *Mandela's Way: Lessons on Life, Love, and Courage* (New York: Crown, 2010), 16. See also Nadine Gordimer, *Living in Hope and History* (London: Bloomsbury, 1999), and Daniel Roux, "Mandela Writing/Writing Mandela," in *The Cambridge Companion to Nelson Mandela*, 205–23 (New York: Cambridge University Press, 2014).

in keeping with Madiba's own sensibility to treat this disclosure as simply another iteration of his political practice. Which is to say, recording and reporting his dream-life was just one more means to regulate and transform the constituent force of the political regime, a means to establish and preserve his own sense of sovereignty against apartheid's imposing force. Dream-life was one more venue Mandela used to exercise his indivisible sense of freedom.

Attending to one's dream-life as a form of political practice is not so much a new idea as a very old one. As the French philosopher and historian Michel Foucault has shown, the ancient Greeks commonly exercised their civic liberty through a series of practical exercises—including dream interpretation. The exercises were sometimes formal practices, such as pedagogical dialogue and examining one's conscience (which would later become confession under Christianity), but they also included everyday gestures, such as style of dress, appearance, and gait. Near the end of his career, Foucault began a concerted investigation of these ancient "techniques of self" to grasp how the individual subject is able to constitute herself in a way that is not reducible to external forms of domination. The project was ultimately left unfinished at the time of Foucault's death, but it nevertheless opened up a different dimension of political subjectivity, a new approach to thinking about the territory of political life that drew from the inside of thought.[4]

One way that Foucault attempted to articulate this other

4. Shortly before his death in 1984, Foucault spoke of an idea for a new book on "technologies of the self." He gave several lectures on the topic, including a seminar presented at the University of Vermont in fall 1982. A partial record of the seminar is published in *Technologies of the Self: A Seminar with Michel Foucault,* ed. Luther H. Martin, Huck Gutman, and Patrick H. Hutton (London: Tavistock, 1988).

dimension of political life was through a distinction he made between the process of liberation and what he called "practices of freedom":

> When a colonized people attempts to liberate itself from its colonizers, this is a process of liberation in the strict sense. But we know very well, and moreover in this specific case, that this process of liberation is not in itself sufficient to define the *practices of freedom* that will still be needed if this people, this society, and these individuals are to be able to define admissible and acceptable forms of existence or political society.[5]

This distinction directly echoes the position Mandela takes at the end of his autobiography, that closing note of hesitation in which the leader troubles the idea that freedom was achieved in South Africa with the advent of democracy. Neither thinker downplays the significance of liberation, but neither sees such victories as sufficient: liberation cannot define or even guide all the practical forms of freedom that will be needed for a viable life. As Mandela puts it, liberation is "the right not to be oppressed," but this is only the first step on a much harder and longer road: "to be free is not merely to cast off one's chains, but to live in a way that respects and enhances the freedom of others."[6]

In the ancient world, one of the most common ways to practice freedom in an everyday sense was through dream interpretation. Foucault's last work, *The Care of the Self,* opens with an extended discussion of the ancient methods of oneirocriticism. Gods gave advice, guidance, and, sometimes, explicit

5. Michel Foucault, "The Ethics of the Concern of the Self as a Practice of Freedom," in *Ethics: Subjectivity and Truth,* ed. Paul Rabinow, trans. Robert Hurley et al. (New York: New Press, 1997), 283–84.

6. Mandela, *Long Walk to Freedom,* 624–25.

commands through dreams. For the ancients, these events constituted a form of guidance, and a high value was set on their decipherment. It was necessary to consult the countless professionals of nocturnal images, and it was also good to be able to interpret these signs for oneself, whether one was rich or poor, old or young, man or woman, private citizen or public official. Learning how to decipher these experiences was necessary to one's freedom, not because it somehow enabled one to get the better of destiny, but rather so one could weather the sufferings that would inevitably come. As one ancient writer put it, "when disasters come altogether and unexpectedly, they strike the spirit with so severe and sudden a blow that they overwhelm it; while if they are anticipated, the mind, by dwelling on them beforehand, is able little by little to turn the edge of sorrow."[7]

Dreaming provided a means for the dreamer to reflect on such disasters and to contemplate her social existence. For the ancients, interpreting these nocturnal events was not a narcissistic exercise of introspection but an everyday means to carry out an examination of one's social moorings. Dreams display one's "style of activity," the position one tends to take with regard to others, indeed, one's larger way of being.[8] Reflecting on these thought-events provides a means to discover and reaffirm one's relation to oneself and to the world. Similar to the way external power relations are imposed through repeated coercive action, so the relation to oneself, which can bend these power relations, is established by practical exercises of freedom—everyday practices that a person might use to hone her relationship with herself.

Mandela's recurring nightmare was not a singular avowal in

7. Achilles Tatius, *The Adventures of Leucippe and Clitophon,* cited in Michel Foucault, *The Care of the Self,* vol. 3 of *The History of Sexuality,* trans. Robert Hurley (New York: Vintage, 1988), 5.

8. Foucault, *Care of the Self,* 35.

this respect. He regularly reported his dreams to his circle of comrades in prison; he shared them in letters to his intimates; he recorded them in his notebooks; he even jotted them down on the annual desk calendars that he used in the period from 1976 to 1989:

8 DECEMBER 1976
Begin reading "Bury my heart" Dee Brown; sent letter U[niversity of] London

23 DECEMBER 1976
Zindzi's birthday

17 JANUARY 1977
Gossiping about others is certainly a vice, a virtue when about oneself.

20 JANUARY 1977
Dreamt of Kgatho falling into ditch and injuring leg

21 FEBRUARY 1977
Raid by approximately 15 warders under W/O Barnard[9]

These occasional entries represent another forum in which Mandela practiced his unique brand of civil disobedience, a quotidian technique he used to reinsert himself into the human condition. Rather than treat his inner landscape as somehow irrelevant to his political life, Mandela constantly reinvented himself by turning the immediate condition of his unfreedom

9. Mandela kept a series of desk calendars on Robben Island and in Pollsmoor and Victor Verster prisons, which run from 1976 to 1989. These particular entries are reprinted in Mandela, *Conversations with Myself,* 267–68. The calendars and other items can be viewed at the Nelson Mandela Centre of Memory, http://www.archive.nelsonmadela.org/.

back upon itself. By drawing from and nurturing that dimension of political subjectivity that is irreducible to the power relations imposed by the state, he continually found ways to fold the force of apartheid, even as it remained a force.

This is one more lesson that the great leader bequeathed to us: our relationship to others ultimately begins with the relationship one has with one's self. Attending to our dream-life is among our most intimate means of tending this relationship, a technique of self-determination, a daily means to practice self-governance, indeed, a paragon of freedom.

Dream Matters

THE SIGNIFICANCE OF DREAM-LIFE has been slowly eroded throughout modernity. It is as if, in some strange way, this era's potent fantasies of rationalization, technological progress, and perfectibility have claimed center stage, displacing the older image of the human being as a small, frangible creature that sleeps and dreams.

But dream we do. And Mandela's example reminds us of the significance of attending to this alternative thought-landscape—especially in dark times. There was little that was secret about the institution of apartheid in South Africa. Yet, paradoxically, this methodical form of political violence was by no means visible to all, nor was it easy to perceive. This is because in such eras, violence is camouflaged by "the highly efficient talk and double-talk" of official representatives, who, "in many ingenious variations, explain away unpleasant facts and justified concerns."[1] Dark times are moments when political violence occurs in full

---

1. Hannah Arendt, *Men in Dark Times* (New York: Harcourt Brace, 1968), viii. As Arendt acknowledges, "dark times" is a phrase borrowed from Bertolt Brecht's poem "To Posterity." Scott Horton provides an original translation and discussion of Brecht's poem on *Harper's Blog*, January 15, 2008, http://harpers.org/blog/2008/01/brecht-to-those-who-follow-in-our-wake/.

view of the public realm, indeed, moments when this sphere of appearances is itself infected by a kind of black light. In these unyielding climates, language is no longer used to disclose and expose but to obfuscate and hide what is. In dark times, under the pretext of upholding old truths, a kind of official language emerges, a vehicle that is designed to degrade truth, to sanction ignorance and preserve privilege, to stall conscience and thwart our capacity to think.

As Madiba taught us, dream-life becomes a particularly potent resource in such climates. The disclosure of his recurring nightmare quietly assures us that *dream-life matters*—it matters both for the individual and for our shared political lives. These uncanny mental events are vehicles for otherwise unthinkable thoughts and a wellspring for the freedom of speech. Dreaming is an indispensable species of psychological work that can help transfigure the force of a harsh reality. These thought-events are one of the principal means of transport for a unique form of knowledge that each subject carries but that remains vexingly other.

Dreams animate human life; that is their work. As Mandela's example shows, disclosing these events can become a political exercise that carries great force. In our own dark times, attending to this alternative form of thinking can perhaps help us live through, resist, and ultimately transfigure our shared social and political landscapes *otherwise.*

Acknowledgments

An early version of this material was presented at a workshop at York University called "Affecting Education: Psychosocial Studies of the Human Condition." I thank Deborah Britzman and the other presenters for helping me hone my argument. My gratitude also goes to Melissa Adler, David Clark, Sarah Freke, Alice Pitt, and Carol Zemel, who, each in his or her own way, encouraged and influenced my thinking. This research was supported by the Social Sciences and Humanities Research Council of Canada.

Sharon Sliwinski is associate professor in the Faculty of Information and Media Studies and the Centre for the Study of Theory and Criticism at the University of Western Ontario in Canada. She is author of *Human Rights in Camera* (2011).